Becoming Sky

Poems

Joseph Hardy

Bambaz Press
Los Angeles 2023

For those who are remembered in these pages
and for John Eichinger, (1952-2023)

CONTENTS

This Moment

Here Between

HERE

not at the first
or last.

lately without a name
or face

leaves turning.
the song right

everything
emptying into my eyes

running over
memory too
spilling

on a table like wine
down the drain forgotten

but here
in this time between
ordinary love.

TRIAL AND ERROR

It's rained for two days,
hard enough to raise the creek,
run it dirt brown

under broken weeds
and algae blooms that swirl past
like gathered cobwebs.

Branches, pulled from banks,
turn like wheels
as they pass.

A helmet-shaped turtle
resists by slow inches, pushes into
half-submerged grass on a mud bank,

but no sign of the baby snappers
I've watched for two weeks
since my dog passed.

No sign of their angled shells
and armored bumps,
perfect in teaspoon miniature,

surely prepared for this by nature,
by the recombinant guessing
of our long and shared inheritance,

trying and erring
through regular disasters.
If not swept away, maybe hidden.

COMPLICITY

I peed my pants in second grade, standing
at one of those rectangular tables for arts and crafts
beside a blond girl whose face I can't remember.

She shouted in disgust, seeing her shoes in a yellow pool.

But before that, I remember the impossible moment
the warm flood broke loose, the one or two frantic seconds
in anguish, when I was able to hold it back, before—
immense,

it overcame me, claimed my leg, my jeans, my left sock
and sneaker. Spilled out onto the tiled floor
while I stood rooted.

I do not remember deciding, only stepping
to the right, pretending it hadn't happened.

That and the worst of it, when I stood in urine-soaked
jeans and maintained, "It wasn't me. I didn't do it."

Humiliation needing my complicity to be complete.

As we lived across the street from school,
I was encouraged to walk home to change.
Once out of sight, I ran.

On my return, hesitating outside, one hand on the
doorknob, I heard a friend ask, "But why would he lie?"

I do not remember the teacher's next words, only that they
were wise and kind. As I re-entered, I understood their
silence had been agreed upon in my absence.

BENJAMIN'S LESSONS

I missed Benjamin today
a first-grader I help with reading
who likes poop-jokes.

They tend to begin like this—*Benjamin*
if you gave this U.S. State a nickname
what would it be?

       "Poop"   he says.
       Sometimes   "Butt."

At the end of our half hour
Benjamin likes to draw mazes
I can't get out of.

He closes the exit
       with his magic marker
              just before I get there.

Or draws the triangular   symbol of poop
       and leaves me
              in the middle of it
                  to teach me
       how it feels to be powerless.

Having learned this as a child
I understand when he asks
completing a work-book page

       "Can I   Benjamin-Scribble it?"

With my approval   he blots-out every
       single question
              and all of his answers,
                  all correct.

WITH TIME

I've lost my everything,
my yin, my yang, my something else
forgotten, except for odd details:

a dirty joke—the first I heard
in a schoolyard, before I knew a speck
about intimacy. The whirl

within those tubs at carnivals—clouds
of candy gossamer forming around
a cardboard cone from almost nothing,

its sticky melting dissonance on teeth,
pink as that fluffy fiberglass insulation
that slowly causes lung disease,

a bit like the sugar-insulation we spin
cocooning kids from life. Useless,
but we can't stop. Or that

unsettled moment a waiter asks,
"How delicious was it?"
and I lie.

Which feels like I took the card
a magician pushed when he said,
"Pick any card."

Instead, I should have listened
with my elbow, as improv teaches.
Met the world

with my funny bone. Accepted all
the unintentional and unexpected,
tingling pain with numb.

Seen the peril of how I sat on top
a Ferris wheel—people below
safe as distant ants.

How I tried to reduce ocean waves
to wrinkles. Avoid the undertow.
Escape the smash and tumult—

heedless of me standing in its way.

Like love, that once announced
itself inside me, and I realized,
I love her, I would

do anything for her—powerless
to deny it, as though I myself
was a gathering wave.

Beginnings

SOMETIMES STRANGERS WOULD APPLAUD

As a child, I thought if I could understand my mother's
hands, I'd understand our troubles. They never stopped,
never rested, flitted like a bird with no safe place to land.

Twitched imaginary lint from a lapel before tugging it
straight. Brushed off nothing from a shoulder as if it were
something. Not just for me, but strangers—all the while
conversing,

juggling: a prying question, an amusing anecdote,
an off-color joke, a snatch of a song to distract or
entertain—more balls in the air than they could count.

Then, just as they decided she'd missed their answers
to the overly personal questions, had let them fall unheard
to the ground,

she'd bring them back, woven in the pattern of her
patter—hands fluttering stops and starts.

TINNITUS

our mother taught us neglect
is a hole in the air,
an unpredictable vacancy of mind.

I have wanted to share it for years
as the taste of something awful,
but it resists conveyance.

like the sound of my sister's tinnitus—
mine, a thin blade bowing the edge
of an unforgiving file—hers

I couldn't say, only
that as a child, sometimes
it kept her from sleeping;

perhaps that sound a freight train makes,
steel wheels repolishing the rails
on a slow curve.

years ago, I lived above those tracks,
bedroom window yards
from sixteen trains a day—

and truly
like neglect
within a week unheard,

except for long nights, in bed with flu or ache
at 2:05 a.m. when the stuttering laden cars
rolled south, squealing their long complaint.

one hundred and sixty-four I counted once
going somewhere, carrying something,
out of mind any other time, yet there.

leaving me in need, wanting
all these disconnected years
a new way of speaking;

the poetry a child expresses
stunned by a sharp and sudden pain
whose mouth opens

in a silent O we hear,
we've all heard
before the shriek,

like my sister once
holding my mother's head against her own
and asking, "Can't you hear it?"

ON THE BIG CHAIR

At a children's table, I bring sharpened pencils.
Keep track of our time and wonder, always,
how I can help these flowering spirits.

Some trust too quickly; it triggers a moment's
panic. Others know an unsafe world already,
but at odd moments even these will share.

Reveal troubles at home.
Present harsh facts of their lives,
then wait

as if asking,
*Is this right? Is this
the way it's supposed to be?*

They hope. Can be delighted. Proud
of mastering what was inexplicable
a few days before.

One makes up stories. Draws red fire
and blue water monsters he defeats
after they've eaten everything in sight.

Another pats my shoulder. "Don't worry,"
she tells me, as her class heads out for a field trip,
"I'll see you next week."

The smallest often says she's hungry. Pretends
to sleep at the table. Seems to be waiting
for adults to settle so she can wake.

ON SATURDAY MORNINGS

when he was off the road from selling,
our cartoons were sometimes interrupted.

Sick at what he saw, or possibly from
an indignity suffered at work, my father
would rectify his life with his hands,

set a short wooden stool in the bathtub
filling with what-felt-scalding water,
say the words, *send one in.*

One at a time, my mother would usher us in,
though she would deprecate this torture
out of earshot, counsel we endure in silence.

I felt but did not understand the rage
constrained in the hot washcloth
scraping dirt from ears,

the disgust, that could have been shame,
in the hand brush pummeling grimy elbows,
grass-stained knees.

Why he'd cut ragged fingernails so tight,
when they'd just regrow. Shove cuticles down
and bark if we jerked.

Eventually, miraculously as if we were
pale crescent moons emerging
under rounded nails, we escaped.

I WISH I KNEW THEIR STORY

On a cold Sunday morning in December, my dog and I found a ball in the park.

A big, thin-skinned ball, under a coating of ice, pink as fresh bubblegum. So vivid, I imagined it bought the day before and left beside the car as a parent rushed a child to go.

A few feet away, a tangled clump of something emerged from snow crust—silver as an astronaut's suit—I told my dog to leave.

On Monday, crows stalked white melting islands on the grass. The ball floated above wood shavings near the swings, borrowed and abandoned.

A child's quilted vest, pristine, shiny as a juice pack, small even for a five-year-old, was hung on the park rules sign. One parent's kind impulse for another, I thought that ran dry, seeing a smaller sodden twin of the vest in the mud beneath.

Tuesday, the two vests gleamed, laid flat on a park bench as if waiting for sale. The ball, stuck beneath a far boundary fence, had shrunken in cold.

Wednesday, one vest had been pushed onto the other to make space for someone to sit. The ball gone.

Receiving Wisdom

RECEIVING WISDOM

I predict, when you're in second grade,
a wise third-grader will share that it's true:

"If you step on a crack,
you'll break your mother's back."

She'll tell you lurid stories about real people,
two different families known by her cousin
in another town, to whom it happened.

And that day, on the half-mile walk from school,
you'll try to miss them all and fail.

You'll race the rest of the way home shaken,
afraid of what you'll find, and learn

what you do,
or fail to do,
will not affect her,

that day no different
than another.

I CAN TELL YOU

Death stands close behind you
in the moment you're told,
"I'm glad I didn't abort you."

You feel him listening, even though
your mother seems pleased she didn't
end you like others she's mentioned.

Until age ten, maybe twelve,
it slightly terrifies each time
she feels compelled to say it,

as though the option
is still open—
only that morning a possibility.

You get older,
perhaps a little braver,
but the worry lingers

and you find yourself asking
at one of those moments,
Why didn't you?

"You were too far along."
she explains. Which finally
settles it.

FEAST DAYS

Somewhere along the way, he determined
he would make his own holidays.

Planted maple trees in Southern California to see
a pale version of the missing red and yellow
leaves of fall in Massachusetts.

Made me stand guard in the aisle of a Rexall drugstore
as he swapped out the red, orange and green bulbs
to make packages of blue.

Hung blue lights on our eaves at Christmas
to remember icicles.

Bought boxes of silver tinsel and instructed us
to throw it like confetti at the tree.

Got the tangled string of lights to work, swearing
violently when he burned his fingers, and in general,
when things did not go well.

He made oyster stew on Christmas eve,
eggnog Christmas day. Set a table of appetizers
in the living room whether we had guests or not.

On the fourth of July, he'd bring out his father's
wooden ladder, gray and speckled with paint drops
hard and multi-colored as sprinkles on ice cream.

Stand it in the middle of our backyard
in front of a semi-circle of aluminum lawn chairs.

He'd drive nails in the ladder to hold pinwheels
that spun like whooshing rockets trying
to escape themselves.

Put two bricks on top to elevate the flare
of each cone-shaped fountain.

Doled out sparklers as it grew dark enough
to write our names in air and see an afterimage
in spitting geometries of fire.

Once, a friend and I pulled a black *Piccolo Pete*
from the fireworks box and crimped it
near the bottom with a pair of pliers.

At the end of its whistling, it exploded
like the most unsuspected and satisfying bomb.

We got the put-your-eye-out lecture, a horrible story
of kids losing fingers.

The exact words are gone from my memory.
What he loved remains.

BEFORE OUR BIRTH

there is a space we wait, some people say.
My shaman friend is certain he was there
and chose to whom he would be born
and for what purpose.

I can only see myself waist-deep
in the ocean, in the hollow of a building wave,
or remember, from this life, an inaudible shudder
that seemed to come from miles beneath

before an earthquake, before
the building shook and floor slid
under my feet. A feeling
of the continent itself being lifted,

carried piggyback, bouncing us
into mid-air like a phonograph needle
jarred from black vinyl
before resettling in a groove.

ECSTASIS

When a friend ran out of space
in every closet in her house, she built
an addition for her clothes:

one large room
like the stores where she shops, four walls,
upper and lower hangers packed.

It's not extravagance. It's impulse—
the same way she adopts dogs,
flooded with compassion.

She's saved seven. Lives with them,
while my love feels a roomful
only randomly leaking out:

a double tip for a harried waitress, an overly long
thank you, embarrassing my wife, for a janitor
whose care wages could not buy.

It's the ecstasy of love, I fear.
Where it could take me.
How it might leave me.

God piling in past my capacity to hold,
pushing me out of myself, as if my body were
a house that could burst with dogs and clothes.

The Job of Children

IT'S THE JOB OF CHILDREN

to reconstruct and make something
trustworthy of their parents.

Like Isaac bound on an altar looking up
into his father's eyes, they must interpret
the knife—

the force of an unexpected slap, which must
mean something, or the lull in an argument
that may precede some violence.

Listen for a meaning behind the meaning.
Invent a history not shared in a handful
of bucolic family stories. Conjure the why

when as a child, a garage door came down on
a cousin's back and as he lay in the driveway
writhing, his mother laughed until breathless.

Fill the gap between them she did not cross
to help. Use words to make up for a lack
persisting to her death.

SHELTER

One of my friends braces himself every morning
on waking—expecting police to knock on his door
to say his son is dead.

Attempted rescue over years, rehabilitation
in different states, all of his offers
of a compromised life, unaccepted.

This, he feels, is rage
expressed in dying.

On her fifth day here, my new puppy
presses against us, sleeps on our feet
as we stand talking, chews a toy

on my leg, looking up
with blue-brown eyes.

My friend places photographs of the child,
the youth, young man on his mantel.

Talks to people in a far city at a homeless shelter
who have seen him, but won't share information,

and a cop—who takes his calls—who told him,
"This is the final spiral of terminal addiction."

He holds his son inside, reading stories
about the lives of street addicts.

MY MOTHER BELIEVED
IN ICE CREAM

Believed it could solve all problems. At least, that is what I thought growing up.

Though I'm not sure what would trigger the impulse, in the middle of a weekday she'd take us to an ice cream parlor.

My older sister and I asked for chocolate, always, but she had difficulty eating hers.

By difficulty, I mean she would either lick the scoop so hard, it would fall to the floor, at which point she would wail. Or lick so slowly, the chocolate would melt all over her hand, all over the half-a-dispenser-full of napkins wrapped around her hand, until at some point she'd drop the slippery mess and wail.

My mother's reaction was instantaneous. She'd snatch the unfinished cone from my hand and shove it into my sister's mouth, silencing her. As money was tight, I seldom got another.

This scene happened enough a cousin told me seeing it changed how she raised her children. Happened enough, I learned to eat ice cream in bites that made my teeth ache. Happened enough on one trip I asked for strawberry instead of chocolate.

My sister ate the strawberry, but said to me, "You should have gotten chocolate."

The next time, I asked for vanilla. It turned out, she wouldn't eat vanilla.

THE SHAPE OF US

Think of how hard it is to find our true shapes:
how we need others and their needs become our own,

how we are malleable and concealed, and the light
within us feels like it comes from someplace else.

Like in my friend who decided, with reason,
he was conceived to be an extra hand
on his parents' farm.

All of his childhood, through high school,
not allowed to sit at the family table and eat
like his sister, given a tray on the floor.

In mid-life, he's begun to paint, extraordinary colors
emerging in common objects: a red curved horn
of a steer, lilac spiral of a dancer's dress.

We who love him wish he would give himself this art—
this completion of love, this radiance of lightning
from the earth to sky.

THERE WERE TIMES

my mother covered the tops of her arms
so bruises didn't show. She confided,
"That's why he hits me there."

It was a cage fight really; he the weaker.
His every punch a question: *Why
don't you love me?*

Hers: "How could I not, dear?"
or, "That didn't hurt."

Perhaps a kabuki play, a ritual seen on nights
that he came home, wound up at work
to stalk a spiral on the living room rug,

working his rage higher and higher, a death-defying
trapeze artist, a tightrope walker, one slip
from disaster.

Sometimes it ended in a private performance
after we were told to go to bed, admissions of pain
wrung from her in their bedroom.

Sometimes it faded—inexplicably—into silence,
a gun brought on stage, but never fired
before the final curtain.

Things I Got Used To

IN NATURE

the closest feeling to it might be starving,
a deficit like an empty sack at your center.

Imagine the opposite of a flood,
a famine perhaps, or years it didn't rain,
someone like us, before us, choosing
the harm in it, eating desolation to survive.

Imagine a breaking, unhealed within the body,
so no soul would rest there overnight.

I DROVE BY

not owning the rage, only imagining
the weight of a heavy pipe, swung like an axe
in the dark.

Wondering, *how many blows I would need*
to shatter a bus stop shelter like that, and *how*
could anyone carry such a weapon unremarked.

It wasn't one bus stop that summer.
For weeks, sprays of pebbled glass glittered
on sidewalks on different blocks,

catching my eye, not letting it pass
as it would over the tired women, sitting,
rested bags between work shoes.

I confess. I did nothing with those feelings
that year but buy a mirror from a local artist
who had hurriedly, ahead of city maintenance,

stopped to sweep a pile of the glass
into a cardboard box she kept in her trunk
for art supplies.

Imagine: thick sea-green fragments, set deep
in red adobe, around a mirror's reflection
and you might see how it could hold violence.

The way a trashcan later that summer was held
suspended in air, half-way through
a broken bus stop wall.

COLLEGE CAFETERIA FOOD
WAS DELICIOUS

I know many grow up without enough to eat, but that was not our family.

My mother made my school lunches until I was fifteen, a baloney sandwich with mayo on white bread and chips every day.

I traded with an older kid once, whose mom had made him a golden chicken schmaltz sandwich on pumpernickel. When I bit into that giving congealed unsalted fat—my mouth shuddered.

"A deal's a deal," he said, and ate my lunch and his.

Mom considered simmering water a boil, couldn't or wouldn't wait for it to bubble, but TV dinners saved me. Swanson's Salisbury steak and mashed potatoes, Chung King sweet and sour shrimp, I devoured them, though sometimes, inside the aluminum compartments, they'd be burned black around the edges, a frozen cube of beef-ice or shrimp-ice in their centers.

She said she'd cooked from a cookbook for four weeks once, in college, and realized she could do it if she wanted to. So, I'm thinking, what I saw was a protest, like she was showing up for work, but engaging in a sit-down strike, due to poor wages or horrible working conditions or a terrible grievance never set right.

I DREAMT OF BASEBALL ALL NIGHT

Raced to where the ball would come down.
A place I could hear in the sound as it left the bat,
see in the angle of its ascent, its speed approaching.

The summer of my tenth year, my father hit thousands
of flyballs to me in the park. Taught,

no matter how fast you run arriving, your body stills.
Glove hand, off your shoulder, gives with the impact
as it closes, turning to put your weight behind you,
fingers finding the crossed seams exactly
where your glove was waiting.

I am not a big man, smaller then for my age,
but that summer my coaches kept me on the field
after practice and hit flyballs

as high and far as they could, to watch me get them,
to see me find the place where they would fall,
and pull them down, into the throw.

NIGHT WATCH

Some nights around midnight, woken from dead sleep
by my mother, I'd shake my brother, "Fire Drill.
Get up. We're cleaning the house."

It felt, with his pacing in and out of our bedrooms,
something like a beast to be fed
nothing filled.

Sometimes earlier, I'd see the troubling
sea-wind freshen, whipping up waves
that built to mountains

to batter the house for an hour
or two, or three, but sometimes
I wouldn't.

It was not sadistic.
There was no glee in it.

It was billowing pain, he a sail
that would crack like a whip in gusts,
then stretch tight, caught by it,

driving us before him—
a slap to keep us moving.

Once, the back lawn my brother
had let go for weeks, mowed
in his underwear at one a.m.

Pain, I think now, grieved to make us feel
his wound, acknowledge wrong,
set our offending surfaces right.

WE SELL THOSE UGLY HOUSES
the billboards say they'll buy

the ones we've lived in among garbage bags of
unwashed clothes and dust-bunnies like wispy clouds of
shadow beneath our beds—unnamed dreams left in tired
wallows—and walk around the piles, dropping what was
in our hands, half an eaten sandwich, the unread mail,
closing doors when piles combine to suffocate a room.

Things I Didn't

I HAVE THIS DREAM
they're casting my life story for a movie

and I'm thinking they love my audition,
when the director stands up and says, "Thank you,
but you're not right for the part."

"It needs someone fresh, someone free
to move the story forward,"he says.

He says, "I know you, of all people, will understand,"
and shakes my hand.

But I don't. I don't understand.

Which is why I'm climbing a brick wall in an alley
outside the studio where they're shooting my movie,
when a security guard grabs me from behind,
one hand hooked into the waistband of my jeans,
one locked on a pants cuff, so if I keep climbing,
I could lose my pants.

But I want to be polite, because Raul,
the older guard with thick silver hair,
who's watching, who looks like the wizard
in *The Wizard of Oz*, and Eddie, the younger
bigger uniform holding me in midair,
are always scrupulously polite
and fair every time they catch me.

I try to tell them, *It's my life*,
and project authority hanging there, but
it comes out a whine, and Raul and Eddie
roll their eyes and discuss where to eat lunch
while we wait for the police.

After the restraining order,

the closest I get
is to hide in the crowd on opening night
outside of the ropes of the red carpet
where I tell everyone, anyone who'll listen,
All this buzz, all of this wild anticipation,
is about me,

but the stars who begin to arrive
emerging from black limousines,
beautiful, glamorous, and that director,
never see me behind the flashbulbs,
and it's not until Tuesday
alone at a matinee, I actually see the movie—
which is wonderful, I must say,

though scenes of my life I thought important
were cut, and others I hardly noticed
at the time, captured the meaning.

METEORS

    fall like rain, like visitors
from another planet, like Superman,
faster than a speeding bullet.

Fall, like your love fell on deaf ears
when you weren't watching, just like baseballs
vanish behind a far right-field fence.

They fall through the fiberglass roof
and queen-size mattress of a couple
sleeping in a trailer in the Australian Outback.

Fall with such intent they kill
all the dinosaurs, level Kamchatka, punctuate
the Yucatan Peninsula with beachfront.

Fall as if they have nothing better to do, or are tired of
traveling alone through space in orbit beyond Mars,
and decide they'd rather burn up in Earth's atmosphere
than go on.

Meteors fall like mercy,
like wingless storks bringing fertile DNA
to an inhospitable planet.

Fall like they were emulating spacecraft and forgot
that last step, about deploying parachutes, to swing
down safely to the sea.

They fall instead like dirigibles catching fire,
like planet busters, extinction events
leaving no tomorrow.

Fall like they never existed, or were just
whistling past a graveyard
and disappeared.

I DREAM OF SAYING TO MYSELF

it is way too big for you.
You should feel no shame.

Your feet barely reach the pedals
at their top; hopeless, even sitting off the seat
on the beautiful chromium-red middle bar,
mashing your balls as you try.

Even your sister's longer legs can't stretch
the last two inches to the bottom as she
sets sail from the curb, escapes
with your pride.

Dipping see-saw left then right,
catching the pedals as they rise
for four driveways, five-away, six,
then one more;

using the last, not falling
in a wide wobbly turn,
straightening, gaining
speed toward the street.

You should have been told,
or understood, or remembered:

the car, summoned as if by your wish,
that swept past on a line so exactly
perpendicular to her crossing,
so inevitable, it seemed to happen
seconds before impact,

was really a drunk,
avoiding a ticket on a side street,
on a Saturday morning after Christmas.

TOUCHSTONE

I've misunderstood the word *touchstone* for years,
believed it was a talisman of comfort, not a test.

Something to hold onto, like a compass for a lost hiker,
the spot a ballerina fixes her eyes upon as she spins.

Mine was a mentor in my self-destructive years,
an unlikely, bellowing, uncommonly generous man

unsteady enough to drink himself to death.
He left a wife and three sons but had held steady for me.

It was an unresolved loneliness in him, I think,
a lack of touch I sometimes feel in me,

as though I cut myself loose from Earth
and have been falling upward ever since.

MERCY

I understand it no better now
than that day cars slowed
to edge around a pigeon
rocking on its back
in the intersection,
one unresponsive wing,
one that pumped in starts,
rowing a half-turn on asphalt
each time a few
endless seconds more

when a rusted station wagon stopped
in traffic, and a young man driving
pushed his door open, not to step out
and move the dying bird,
but to look back and see clearly
as he backed his left rear tire
over its head,
then to check again
moving slowly forward
to see it was dead.

Greater Mysteries

THERE'S A GNOSTIC GOSPEL
I've read about

a fragment of papyrus, or
scraped skin severed
just as we

from the holy body of self.
A translation, they believe
from earlier Greek

made sixteen hundred years ago;
this one piece, the title,
all that remains:

A Gospel for Those
Who Feel Strangers in Every Land.
Only that.

No other words needed
perhaps for those like us
empty

who must find
in each wilderness
their own way.

WHAT CAN BE SAVED

A small oil painting of a girl moved with us
each time we moved. Never hung, left on top
of old suitcases or dusty boxes in our garage.

The girl not much more than seven. Black hair,
hacked in a bob. Behind her, swirls of dark paint,
the color of moss.

Her face was pale and freckled. Cheeks, spots
of red, as if rouged, or she'd just run in
from playing outside.

I remember her eyes. Dark eyes that felt to me
like they held something too large inside.

Had I known what beauty was when I was as a child,
I might have called it beautiful.

Once, I asked my mother, *Who is she?*
"Just a girl." she said.

It looks like you. Is it you?
"No."

Sixty years later, canvas cracked, broken,
long since thrown away, my mother said, "Dear,

you should find that painting of me.
It was by a famous painter who visited us
when I was a girl.

It may be worth something."

THERE'S A FEELING
something needs us here

We, who have joined birds and apes
as tool makers, raccoons with opposable thumbs,

who did not invent killing to eat,
parasites, cancer, domination within a pack,

not even the lying
practiced by moths mimicking tree bark;

with the Earth no longer flat, sun
no longer revolving around us, we feel

something needs us here.

UNDER A GREEN MOUND
in Ireland

    another tourist to enter a dark tomb,
I met myself five thousand years ago.

Crouched down to walk a winding path
between gray standing stones I'd raised.

Felt one with those who did—
an urge to sing

the winter solstice, our dark passage,
and the mystery of light,

the days that shorten
pitiless, old bodies shed

and what remains—a gift
which God cannot take back,

if he is bound by love
as we are,

having set in us a slow consuming fire,
our voices swirling sparks born in its heat,

our song in darkness, not as much in faith
as of desire, to remind him we are here.

IN WITNESS

My mother did not speak much of her own childhood, although I did not realize this for years. When asked about it, she would offer a single rosy sentence of an idyllic time, then change the subject, something she was better at than anyone I ever met.

Given the slightest opportunity, she also tended to lie about the consequential and inconsequential, to say something you might like better than how things really were. This was reflexive, so ingrained it might have happened without her conscious thought.

Strangely then, almost all I know about my father's childhood—his illnesses, being made to sleep in a crib until he was five, his mother's attempted suicide, come from stories told by my mother. Stories she must have learned from him or his mother, stories I trust because they were told by a voice inside her that never lied.

The voice was not hers exactly, its intonation flatter, slightly cynical, mildly amused, an observer somehow separate from the rest of her, that would comment thoughtfully on how the world worked and the odd ways people behaved, and objectively critique even her own worst behavior, accurately predicting bad outcomes.

But whatever this observer knew about my mother, it did not change how she lived. It was as if this part of her did not speak to the rest of her.

What I came to believe, the best I could come up with as a child, was she was like an exploded planet whose pieces needed to be kept apart, whirling in orbit around each other, that if those pieces ever came together—were allowed to touch—conscious of all the other pieces at once, something terrible would happen.

I WISH ONE WORD

    of the 171,476 in the English language was useful
in describing us: *haphazard* maybe, maybe *destined*,
unfolded like a leaf in spring (the strength of which,
opening, cannot be doubted),

peripatetic, a bumblebee's flight, a damselfly's dancing
above water in sunlight, *purposeful* as a long line of ants
toward food, or *frantic* as them carrying away eggs
from an uncovered nest.

I do not mean to strand you in ambiguity,
or cheer my own ignorance, or ask you
to quote scripture, or remind me how often
I hide from unpleasant facts.

I acknowledge the Sufi proverb:
A pebble is small,
but what can you see
if you hold it in front of your eye?

And perhaps, if we cannot encompass our meaning,
the only help is an odd tenderness
toward ourselves, an unfounded trust
in our imperfect knowing.

RAIN, LIKE IDLE FINGERS

might sound, tapping a metal bucket,
for all of the lack of sun this morning,
no heavier than that.
God's not into dramatics today.
No fire and brimstone.
No rending of earth as when Jesus died.
No storm lashing Adam and Eve out of Eden.
No cataclysmic meteor striking the Yucatan
to extinguish the dinosaurs.
No glacial sheet of ice overwhelming Europe
to drive the Neanderthals south.
A day of forgiveness perhaps,
an intermission.

Things that Didn't Work

YOU MIGHT FIND IT HELPFUL

to keep embarrassing loneliness
behind the board games on a closet shelf
too high for anyone to see.

A cardboard box is best, wrapped
in anonymous brown butcher paper,
tied securely with twine.

I think of mine as a present
for a future day, an unwritten diary
for my heirs to find.

Unfair to them I suppose,
but some things are harder to throw away
than others.

One difficulty,
it sometimes weeps, seeping out
to soak Monopoly and Clue,

no longer held incoherent
in dreams I forget
in the first blink of waking.

MY OLD BUSHIDO
no longer carries me

Although I did not know the word then,
it was a promise I made to myself as a child.

Something I found in boys' books, written
decades before I was born, of heroes

who spoke of *pluck* and *grit* and unsparing
humility that would win the day.

Stripped down, it had the chill beauty
of polished steel. Was guiltless in its poverty.

Meant nothing could touch me.
Nothing would be enough.

Useful, I found, in schoolyards
where boys make rules and choose sides

and years later, navigating faceless buildings
where money and meaning are confused.

But now, more like a faithful old sedan, a Buick
or Lincoln Town Car, left up on cinder blocks.

Something I maintained with pride for years
then abandoned, wanting more.

Wanting someone closer
than its clean and soothing emptiness.

QUERENCIA

Some mornings, I try to find my shape
and don't know where to start:

from my feet up, or insides out,
from yesterday's shape if I can remember it.

Mirrors aren't much help.

More often now, I hope I form
from kindness, from sympathy.

Imagine myself as a bull that's found
no way out of the ring and accepted, finally,

the number of goading lances, wounding barbs
and deft *verónicas* of empty cape he needed
to stop blindly charging and face who he is.

Querencia, Hemingway called it,
the place where the bull finds his courage,

and with it, it seems, the necessary knowledge
of a stunted life before.

BRILLIANT

At twelve, I had an idea that I could fix my mother. That I could ask for stories of her life, make her tell me the truth, listen and hold the most awful parts of her while she spoke, along with the good parts, and somehow put her back together.

It wasn't well thought out, more an intuition of what she was inside, and my own need to have her whole.

When she caught on, or whatever part of her that protected her from this happening caught on to what I was trying to do, she told me this story···

You know I've had three abortions.

When your father took me to Tijuana for the third one, he took me upstairs to a place that looked like a dirty dentist's office, then he left me there with the abortionist, a man with a big white beard like Santa Claus, and went to get drunk at a bar on the corner.

Before we started, the man said to me, "You are very beautiful. I am very attracted to you. Since you are going to have the abortion, and you will not be able to get pregnant from me, I would like to have sex first."

I was horrified and refused. He did the abortion, but I lost a lot of blood and got sepsis, a bad infection. I almost died. I was pale sick for the next six months.

I remembered those months, her blanched-faced weakness when I was very young, weeks of disappearing into her bedroom, although I had had no idea what it meant at the time.

I remember, as she finished this story—looking at her, thinking, you win.

ZOMBIE LIFE

Think of me as an unshriven ghost at your banquet,
a scuttling remnant of hunger

following you
around the dining room table,

broadcasting like an ice cream truck
playing a jingle around the block:

> *Let me tell you what my mother*
> *my father did—show you my childhood scars*

> *tell you how I cared for my husband*
> *my wife, before I was abandoned,*

all hurt, all abuse melting into one blind sound
seeking any ear but my own.

Enough Sadness for All

I DON'T BELIEVE SHE
WAS THE ONLY ONE

    that girl I saw touching up her lipstick,
singing to the mirror of circling men,

the one who learned in her body she
was irresistible, long before understanding,

and could suspend gravity
for minutes at a time

protecting those she loved

with impromptu show tunes and the cheerful
misdirection of a magician's assistant.

She was the girl I knew, who brimmed
with love and guilt for children

she kept in her heart, but sometimes misplaced,

who seemed to float

among the homeless as a sister,
but not indulge her own regrets,

who gave the rent to sad-eyed panhandlers
and telemarketing charities
and anyone who asked.

She was that girl who knew
completely

there would always be someone
she should please
whom she'd let down,
no matter what she gave—

like the silence she gave her family,

who looked away
when she was her father's favorite.

BROKEN WINDOW

in sleep
      a wind blows through me
broken   window

dew drifts in
      night leaks out

moisture on walls
the floor
my bed.

a mosquito's sour hum
nears

sluggish fears trail   wet
      across the blanket

in my dreams someone
      almost catches   someone

i sit down
      with strangers to eat

the past recedes

nothing
has replaced it

ENDINGS

After rolling tight the towels she had gathered from
around the apartment, she wedged them underneath every
window and door so no air could get in and prevent her
suicide. Turned off the stove's pilot light, turned the gas
high, and laid down on the floor of their kitchen.

It must have been the end of her world, narrowed down to
just her dying, no thought beyond. Unlikely she envisioned
her family finding her dead. Unlikely she considered a
spark might ignite the gas filling the apartment after her
death, that could destroy the home of her three remaining
sons and husband.

It was the loss of her oldest son at twenty-one, unexpected
love in a hard life. Asleep in the back seat, he died in
an automobile accident coming home from college with
friends. A truck driver, nodding off, crossed the divide of
the road.

Thinking everyone still at the wake, she stole out early and
prepared her death, unaware her youngest son, nine years
old, had preceded her home. My father was in his bed
when he smelled the gas.

He came downstairs, turned the stove knobs to off,
opened the doors and windows, and dragged her slight
unconscious body out onto their front lawn. He was still
alone with her on the lawn when she woke.

She raged at him. Struck his face. Told him he had no
right to interfere. Said what he had always felt, unspoken.
"I never wanted you. I never wanted any of you except
him."

GRANADA

Years after his death,
reminded by me of her infidelities,

my mother shared my father's periodic
intoxication with certain songs:

Ray Conniff's "Baubles, Bangles, and Beads,"
Peter Nero's "Mountain Greenery,"

and seven or eight versions of "Granada,"
he had me record on an 8-track tape
to play continuously,

were each connected to a girlfriend
he'd had at the time.

Songs I remember filling our house
on weekends he was happiest.

IN LATE AFTERNOON

after his first congestive heart failure,
I found my father asleep in his bedroom,

no longer theirs, my mother sleeping
in a room down the hall,

his breathing, bubbling gurgles, the musky scent
of him overpowering in near dark

shaded by oleanders and bottle brush
he'd planted for privacy the year he bought the house.

Sweat saturated a towel on pillows
propping him up so he wouldn't drown.

The damage of childhood he drank to numb
and the toll of drinking becoming one thing

less important over time, like the name of a town
where you grew up, a car you once owned.

ONE MORE THING ABOUT
ICE CREAM

I've come to believe, after trips
to the tree-shaded pasture out in the country
where her family picnicked

where her mother and father
would lay out a blanket and tell their children
to find other places to play,

when as a child, only my mother
and her father were there—
ice cream

on the trip back to town
was salve for an impaling
gag for her scream.

Enough Grace

STARDUST

I think of our wandering
out of the rift, walking on savanna
spreading out across sand and ice.

I think of the heart given that we
would feel something missing,
flowers found in Neanderthal graves,

the pain of the world born in us
minor creations, creation revisited
to give the joy of it.

Not lost.
How we were made
to find each other.

FOR ONE ON A LEDGE

I believe
you're listening
to the wrong part of you.

Feel the cold,
your hunger, the need
to come inside
instead.

Allow a restart.
Take another turn.
Wake in another day
of unsorted horseshit—
the diamond-hard crippler
unresolved
in the middle.

Stall for time
while drama
wanders off
to get a latte.

Waiting
is all it takes,
one breath to the next.

CELESTIAL NAVIGATION

Sometimes you lose yourself
when a spouse dies

or a child, who had anchored
meaning, leaves.

Sometimes it's arriving
at a destination that had relegated

everything else in your life
to the wake behind.

Echoes cease. The stars
themselves are gone from the night sky.

There's nothing left to find a bearing

only dips and swells
of internal tides,

only the yaw
of you, always there.

LISTEN

a voice will find you—
divide silence like a body emerging
from a river in moonlight.

You will have no name.
Not need the language
of strangers to speak.

Some things
will become certain.
Shoes for your feet.

You'll walk.
The sun and sky then stars
the moon

a reflection
of light unguarded,
an exhalation of light.

IN A WEEK OF SUN

We crowbar up and dumpster long stretches of rot,
the whole surface of a friend's old deck,
pulling every stranded nail.

The new sixteen-foot planks, two grades below
perfect, warped, need our legs to push
to straighten as we screw them into joists.

Every cloud passing, any breeze brings relief.
My hat drips sweat for five days
and I feel nirvana

shaping this weathering bit of human perspective
straight lines of boards, straight lines of
space between, something on which to stand.

I CAN'T DANCE
and it's too wet to plow

    but it's time to unlimber, get
the lead out, leave misgivings at the door,
fill our lungs with air before diving into
a cold river. Leap.

There's too much joy not to dance.
We are empty mason jars, wine glasses
left out in the yard after a party,
filling with rain.

This Moment

THIS MOMENT
WITH PICK AND SHOVEL, HERE

is a long way
from wherever I've been,
an odd time to feel present,

like the man who jumped
from the Golden Gate Bridge
realizing in that second

he didn't have to.
There was nothing in his life
he couldn't fix.

Here I break the hard ground,
plow long crooked furrows
I love instead of straighten.

Plant a little peace,
some easiness, a seed of hope.
Offer a silent ceremony

for each weed I remove to honor
how preposterously strong
it grew in stone.

This moment with pick, with shovel,
a hoe of sorts, I make a space
for lilies of the field.

SHE WAS CRACKED

and love ran out of her, sometimes
to where it was needed. Which seemed
no blessing to her, as she was always leaking:

money, off-color jokes, bits of love songs
she would hum before singing a favorite line,
and hopeless romance—the least likely, the best.

Like a nursing mother's milk spreading out
through her blouse, a broken bottle pouring wine
into the street, it was nothing she could stop.

Which may be how the world itself began:
the first mother breaking open to empty herself
of blue oceans,

her final breaths becoming sky,
her slackening body left behind
as a lasting remembrance for her children.

NIGHT SKIES

Flowers find their own sun no matter where planted.
The odd weed takes the best place for itself.

My grandchildren turned out to be themselves,
our connection more a gate

that let me in to tend them
and out to let them grow.

They are in their supple years, all possibility, ignorance
and grace—in wet spring, early summer of sun.

They flourish without me.
Pat me on the head in visits

but keep me in their night skies
a once wished-upon star, a background constellation

needed for their story, a memory we share
of them leaning against me.

HAPPENSTANCE

My friend's backyard has become a refuge for gypsies:
feathered travelers, fireflies—migrating spirits
on this plane and the next.

A bullfrog found a way through a wooden fence
into his new pond, buzzing life to the grass
and trees beyond.

He's a man who carries his hometown tattooed
under his skin, the stories of people he loves
told in their own voices,

those who made and rejected him
in a single breath, set him to wandering,
led him to marry the world instead.

ACKNOWLEDGMENTS

I wish to thank the editors of the following literary journals where these poems first appeared, some slightly revised or titled differently:

"Mercy" in *Appalachian Review*, "Tinnitus" in *Bamboo Ridge*, "I Wish One Word" and "Touchstone" in *Cold Mountain Review*, "I Dream of Saying" in *Connecticut River Review*, "In a Week of Sun" in *Constellations*, "There's a Feeling Something Needs Us Here" in *decomp journal*, "I Drove By" in *Dunes Review*, "The Shape of Us" in *Greatest City Diary*, "This Moment with Pick with Shovel" in *Havik*, "Feast Days" and "In Late Afternoon" in *Hole in the Head Review*, "For One on a Ledge" (titled "Advice to Those About to Jump") and "College Cafeteria Food Was Delicious" in *In Parentheses*, "I Wish I Knew Their Story" in *New Writing Scotland*, "Shelter" in *Plainsongs Poetry Magazine*, "I Can't Dance" in *Poet Lore*, "My Mother Believed in Ice Cream," (titled "How I Learned to Love Vanilla") in *Quiet Lightning*, "I Sit on the Big Chair" in *Scapegoat Review*, "Endings" in *SHARE Journal*, "It's the Job of Children" in *Sheepshead Review*, "Granada" in *Sheila-Na-Gig*, "Receiving Wisdom" in *Structo*, "Happenstance" in *The Bookends Review*, "In Nature" in *The Concrete Desert Review*, "We Sell Those Ugly Houses" in *The Courtship of Winds*, "Zombie Life" in *The Dillydoun Review*, "Night Skies" in *The Rainbow Poems*, "Broken Window" in *The Stillwater Review*, "Trial and Error" in *Third Wednesday*, "My Old Bushido" in *Twisted Vine Lit Arts Journal*, "Rain, Like Idle Fingers" in *Rue Scribe*, "Listen," "There's a Gnostic Gospel," and "Under a Green Mound" in *Unleash Press*, "Benjamin's Lessons" and "I Have This Dream" in *Variant Literature*, "Complicity" in *Waving Hands Review*, "Ecstasis" in *You Might Need to Hear This*.

I am grateful for the generosity of the poets and teachers who encouraged and guided me in the completion of this book (in order of their help): Charles Hargett, Dr. Stellasue Lee, Dr. Gary McDowell, Darnell Arnoult, and Linda Parsons. Any awkwardness that remains in the writing after their help is irremediably mine.

I would also like to thank The Porch non-profit writing collective in Nashville, Tennessee, for their many fine classes, for the opportunity to learn and now teach there.

The layout of this book is done by Dr. Baz Here, poet and sculptor, in whose hands your work is always safe. Thank you, Baz.

ABOUT THE COVER

The cover of my book is an oil painting on wood by Rob Douglas, known as Robbie to his friends. Before me now, the painting is titled *Inchoate Form*.

> A figure at the base, three brushstrokes of green,
> looks up into the painting itself, like a man raising
> his arms, witnessing night and day and the moon's
> transit all at once, at that moment part of everything.

In Denver, in half an old gas station Rob rented as a studio and home, he built a temporary wall twelve-feet high, sixteen-feet across, to separate his bed and hot plate from his work.

Something in him compelled him to paint the huge wall as though it were a canvas, and having spilled paint, to paint the cold concrete floor itself.

The wall and floor, like his paintings, had a depth of color I could not grasp, no fixed point at which my eye could stop, no way to take it all in. So beautiful, I found myself reluctant to step on the floor when he invited us in.

I chose this painting as the cover for my book because Robbie, whose life was not easy, expressed the light within himself as beauty to be shared.

WHAT ROBBIE WROTE
ABOUT HIS WORK

*My intention is to move the viewer into another reality—
into a reality beyond the non-representational world of
abstract painting. It is my desire to bring the viewer into
an inviting place of familiarity and contemplation.*

*I achieve to accomplish this process with the intuitive
application of geometric forms as the foundation on
which amorphous objects and forms and defined spatial
planes interact together. Too, the rich surfaces of the
paintings are saturated with infinite details involving
delicate pigment washes and markings.*

*It is in this interaction of these spatial planes and various
elements that may create a sense of place. It is my hope
that the inspired imagery will evoke an emotional response
to a place we have never seen, but yet we know somehow
and find familiar.*

Rob Douglas (1960-2017)

ABOUT THE AUTHOR

Joseph Hardy lives in Nashville, Tennessee, with his wife of thirty-five years, Judith, and their dog, Charley Girl. They are fortunate to have a large circle of friends that includes: a shaman, some songwriters, musicians, singers, authors and playwrights, a few counselors, one or two movers and shakers, several fine cooks, one with exceptional children, and a loving family that is spread across the country and now extends to great-grandchildren.

His first book of poetry, *The Only Light Coming In*, was published by Bambaz Press in 2020. A picture book, *At the Reading of the Will*, written in collaboration with the artist, ED Hose and with the layout design of Charles Royce, IngramSpark 2023.

www.ingramcontent.com/pod-product-compliance
Lightning Source LLC
Chambersburg PA
CBHW032020090426
42741CB00006B/677